Getting More Out of the Eucharist

SOMETHING MORE FAITH SERIES

Mark Hart, Series Editor

theWORD
among us®
press

Published by The Word Among Us Press
7115 Guilford Drive, Suite 100
Frederick, Maryland 21704

23 22 21 20 19   1 2 3 4 5

ISBN: 978-1-59325-001-0

Nihil Obstat: Msgr. Michael Morgan, J.D., J.C.L.
                Censor Librorum
                January 11, 2019

Imprimatur: +Most Rev. Felipe J. Estévez, S.T.D.
                Bishop of St. Augustine
                January 11, 2019

Cover design by Suzanne Earl

Made and printed in the United States of America

Library of Congress Control Number: 2019930339

Contents

Our Spiritual Food

By Fr. John Muir

It's midnight, Christmas Eve Mass. The last hymn for the Communion procession fades into silence. The altar cleared, I sit in the main celebrant's chair and gaze wistfully into the cavernous candlelit church packed with people. I see fathers, mothers, grandparents, teenagers, babies—people from every continent and background. Almost two thousand people, seated in rapt attention. On what, or whom? On the Eucharistic Body of Christ, offered to God and now received sacramentally by almost all of them. Quietly they ponder the One who is laid in a feeding trough—a manger—to be spiritual food for us hungry humans. In that pregnant silence, we worship him who is now one with us.

As I look at this throng of souls in silent prayer, a cynical thought flashes through my pastor's heart: where are so many of them during the *rest* of the year? But suddenly a more useful—but achingly painful—question gently replaces it. A prayer, in fact: what can I do to help them to remain here, in the peace of the Eucharistic Jesus, not just for a few moments but for this whole year?

You hold in your hands an answer to that prayer. This book, *Getting More Out of the Eucharist,* is an energizing and engaging tool for anyone looking to do just that: to get more out of the inexhaustible gift of the Eucharist.

But why read a book about the Eucharist? Shouldn't the Body and Blood of Christ just "work its magic" on us by our showing up at Mass? If the Eucharist is truly the Real Presence of Jesus under the disguises of bread and wine, isn't it enough to simply receive and adore Jesus in the Eucharist? After all, you don't have to know anything about nutrition to get the benefit of a healthy salad. Why should it be any different with the Eucharist?

The answer is that the Eucharist is a *sacrament*. Thomas Aquinas said that all sacraments are "sacred signs." They aren't just holy things but holy *signs*. That means that they *signify*. Signs demands intelligence because they *mean* something you can't see. In this way, sacraments speak a kind of language. And languages require learning—even across a lifetime. Understanding *how* this most blessed of the Church's seven sacraments signifies the reality that it bears—Christ himself—is essential for getting more out of the Eucharist.

In this book, Mark Hart teaches the "language" of the Eucharist to those ready to get more out of this pinnacle form of Catholic prayer. He effortlessly weaves together the simplest of human experiences with the biblical "grammar" that is essential for intelligently grasping the Eucharist more deeply: creation, manna, passover, history, and presence. You will benefit greatly from his fluency in speaking of this greatest of sacraments.

Each session of the book will help you to see, think, and apply this Eucharistic language to your own life and worship. Mark Hart's writing is at once practical and rich. It crackles with the urgency of an evangelist who wants you to know the fire of divine life that burns in his heart. Whether this is the first or the fiftieth book you've read on the Eucharist, it will surely deepen your understanding of the Blessed Sacrament and increase the frequency and quality of your Eucharistic encounters with Our Lord.

In a time when the Church and the world desperately need souls who know, love, and attract others to the Eucharistic Christ—not just once or twice, but throughout the whole year—this book is most welcome. It is an answer to the prayer of this pastor, and of many other hungry hearts.

How to Use This Booklet

Whether used individually or in a small group, each session of *Getting More Out of the Eucharist* is designed to take under an hour. If you use it on your own, remember to begin and end each session with prayer. You might also want to find someone to talk to about what you're learning.

If you are part of a small group, the following guidelines can help you have a fruitful experience:

1. Establish a prayerful environment by taking time to pray before beginning. Ask the Holy Spirit to be with your group. Pray "Come, Holy Spirit" slowly several times. Allow for a few moments of silence. Then say a prayer together, like the Our Father or Hail Mary or Glory Be.

2. Have one or two people read the Scripture passage aloud.

3. Assume everyone has read the commentary beforehand. The group facilitator can ask everyone if this is the case. If it is not, you might want one or two people to summarize the main points or say what most struck them from the reading.

4. Discuss the questions, being careful not to rush to the next one, especially if not everyone has spoken. Some people need more time to gather their thoughts. Some may need a moment of silence before they feel free to express themselves.

5. If the discussion strays, try to bring it back to the questions or the text. Any member of the group should feel free to gently steer the discussion to the next point.

6. When you are finished with the questions, the group facilitator should outline the prayer exercises presented and ask whether anyone has any questions about them. Encourage participants to do the suggested prayer exercises.

7. End with prayer. Perhaps someone could pray spontaneously, thanking God for the opportunity to gather together to pray and study God's word.

8. Make sure you know when and where you are gathering for the next session. Participants will get the most out of each small group session if they read the Scripture passage and commentary and reflect on the questions before the group gathers again.

GET THE MOST OUT OF YOUR BOOKLET

Before each session, visit **wau.org/faithseries** for a short video from the author.

SESSION ONE

Jesus Thirsts for Us

John 15:4

Remain in me, as I remain in you. Just as a branch cannot bear fruit on its own unless it remains on the vine, so neither can you unless you remain in me.

" I want J-e-e-s-us!"

The cry was heard around the church. It echoed off the marble floors, the wooden pew, and the stained glass. The words were as unmistakable as their source: my two-year-old son.

His repeated cries bellowed through the church as we went to Communion, and I felt all eyes upon the two of us. My fellow Mass-goers must have been thinking, "Hey buddy, get that kid under control."

But when I returned, red faced, to my seat, the Holy Spirit intervened, and I realized that something had "stuck" with my son. At all those Masses, I had pointed toward the sanctuary, whispering in his ear, "That's Jesus, right there in the priest's hands."

Have you ever felt the kind of passion, the intense desire for Jesus in the Eucharist that my son expressed so loudly at that Mass?

You may have heard the Church's teaching that the Eucharist is "the source and summit" of the Christian life (*Catechism*, 1324). This means that the Eucharist is the foundation, the root, and the hinge pin upon which every spoke of our faith revolves. It is in the Holy Eucharist that we come to know God most intimately. Why do you think God would command us to set aside the Sabbath each week to enter more perfectly and more fully into relationship with him? Could it be that this is how we "remain," or as some translations say, "abide," in him, as Jesus says in the Gospel of John (15:4)?

God is a Father, and he wants to gather his family at the table to inspire, empower, and strengthen them for the days ahead. He knows that it is only in him that we can truly satiate our deepest hunger. God's greatest desire for us is to experience the depths of his perfect love and mercy.

Why? Because God is the "author of life" (Acts 3:15), the One who imbued us with that very desire for him. This is why C. S. Lewis told us that "If I find in myself a desire which no experience in this world can satisfy, the most probable explanation is that I was made for another world." This is why St. Augustine reminded us that our souls are restless until they rest in him.

At the Beginning

In chapters 1 and 2 of the Book of Genesis, we are given two accounts of creation. In the first, God creates from a distance. He breathes creation into existence. God is a sovereign power, a deity higher than the heavens and, for the most part, unreachable.

In the second creation account, however, the all-powerful Creator draws near to us. He forms man from the earth (Genesis 2:7) and woman from the side of the man (2:21-22). As the story unfolds, the writers of Genesis point us toward important realities. Yes, God is all-powerful and sovereign, but he is also accessible and available to us. God desires a relationship with us, and an intimate relationship at that! We see God enter into a covenant with this first couple, instituting a weekly sabbath day of rest, in which they could enter (and remain) in relationship with their Creator and Father. We see God not only create the garden but walk within it, going so far as to take an evening stroll with the man and woman because he desires to be near his children (3:8).

> God's greatest desire for us is to experience the depths of his perfect love and mercy.

Our heavenly Father is revealing to us that a relationship with him extends far beyond just initial creation. He is revealing that his most ardent, most deep-seated desire for us is rooted in relationship, not merely rituals or rules. He sent his Son to become one of us and to die for our sins. He gave us Jesus in the Eucharist so that he could abide in us and we could abide in him.

God desires us, and he wants us to desire him. If we are not experiencing intimacy with Christ in the Eucharist, then we must ask ourselves if we are in a place to receive his love. Perhaps we are holding on to unreconciled sin. Maybe we feel unworthy. It's possible that we are not taking the time outside of Mass to really get to know Jesus in Scripture. We could be just too busy or distracted. Perhaps we have never just sat with Jesus in Adoration of the Blessed Sacrament and allowed him to gaze upon us in love.

We all struggle with accepting God's love, but if we expand our vision—if we see Christ as the lover of our souls and recognize the sacramental lengths to which he goes to embrace us—our experience of the Eucharist can grow. Perhaps, like the saints before us, we can understand in some small way just how much Jesus thirsts for us.

Questions for Reflection and Discussion

1. Imagine yourself taking an evening stroll with God in a beautiful garden, as Adam and Eve did. What would you say to him? How would he respond?

2. How well do you know Jesus? What time, beyond Sunday Mass, do you spend in conversation with him, getting to know his heart? How often do you pray with the Scriptures?

3. Is Sunday an important day of rest for you? How do you reserve it as time set aside to rest in the peace of Christ?

4. How often do you get distracted at Mass? What could help you to better focus on what's happening on the altar?

5. As we begin this study on the Eucharist, ask yourself, "Does my heart cry out with a desire for Jesus (like my two-year-old) each time I approach the sacrament?" Why or why not?

This week, give yourself some time to do a little self-evaluation. Clear your schedule for at least fifteen minutes, and ask yourself a few simple questions:

- **What is the current source of rest and refreshment that I seek?** Is it Christ, or is it something else? Perhaps you seek rest from a friendship, hobby, or pastime. Take some time to actually name these sources, and seek to answer why you place such an importance on them.

- **What is the destination or summit I fix my eyes upon?** Is it Christ, or is it something else? Perhaps you fix your eyes on a personal goal, a career accomplishment, or simply affirmation from others. Take some time to actually name these destinations, and seek to answer why you place such importance on them.

Close out your time by analyzing your schedule to find a ten-minute block of time each day to commit to prayer. During this time, offer these false sources and summits to Christ. Ask that he perfect your desires and grant you the awareness to see that your longing for rest and fulfillment can only be satisfied in him.

SESSION
TWO

Christ's Life
in You

John 6:47-51, 53-54

"Amen, amen, I say to you, whoever believes has
eternal life. I am the bread of life. Your ancestors
ate the manna in the desert, but they died; this is
the bread that comes down from heaven so that one
may eat it and not die. I am the living bread that
came down from heaven; whoever eats this bread
will live forever; and the bread that I will give is
my flesh for the life of the world." . . . Jesus said to
them, "Amen, amen, I say to you, unless you eat the
flesh of the Son of Man and drink his blood, you
do not have life within you. Whoever eats my flesh
and drinks my blood has eternal life, and I will raise
him on the last day."

"Checkmate," my grandfather said with a wry grin.
My grandfather was many things: wise, jovial,
compassionate, and joyful. But merciful he was
not. He didn't give me any breaks when we played chess. If
I won, it was because I had earned it.

I miss him. Whether in chess or in life, he taught me how
to see the bigger picture, to think ahead, and to begin with
the end in mind.

God the Father is much like that. He invites us to shed our myopic, earthly perspectives and look to our end goal: eternal life with him. God wants us to constantly strive for greater virtue. He never allows us to settle for less than the best version of who he created us to be. He created us to be saints, and he knew we would need his very life to make it happen.

Looking Back and Looking Forward

Before Jesus refers to himself as the Bread of Life in the passage above, he has fed the five thousand (John 6:1-13). He gives the people their dinner so that they don't have to travel a long way, hungry and tired, to get food. Afterward, they seek him out, but he warns them not to go after the "food that perishes" but the food that will last "for eternal life" (6:27).

Jesus also alludes to the time his Father fed the Israelites manna in the desert. Why? He wants them to think back to another time when God fed his people, sustaining them on their long journey. He wants them to look back so that they can appreciate what is ahead. As in chess, the Master is always several moves ahead, even if the pieces have not all fallen into place yet.

During their forty years of wandering in the desert, the Israelites, fearful they would die of starvation, called out to God, and as a good Father, God provided. Each morning, a mysterious white substance appeared on the ground, which they called manna, meaning "What is this?" It was bread-like, edible, and apparently filling.

It's important to note the commands from God that came with the manna. First, it had to be gathered each morning and not hoarded; the Israelites were only to gather the amount they needed for that very day. Second, since God would provide it daily, they were to learn to rely on him constantly. He was teaching them dependence and trust. Third, the day before the Sabbath (Saturday), they were to collect two days' worth of food, so as not to violate the Sabbath—a day about rest and relationship with God. Finally, they were to set aside a jar of manna as a sign for future generations of God's enduring faithfulness. All of these actions demonstrated the desires of God's heart and, ultimately, set the stage for his Eucharistic providence centuries later. God's "daily bread" has its roots in Exodus!

> We need his grace to survive and thrive in this world we live in.

Jesus directs the people to look beyond the physical food they have hungered for and to see instead the eternal life for which they should have been yearning. He calls them to change their lives and perspectives, focusing less on the bread in front of them (the multiplication of the loaves) and more on Jesus himself—the bread that had come down to them. Jesus was offering the people a new perspective.

Jesus' Life in Us

We think of the food we eat as sustaining our lives, but do we ever think of the Eucharist in the same way? The truth is that in the Eucharist, Jesus pours *his* life into us. We received his life when we were baptized. But we all know how challenging life is. We need God's supernatural life flowing in us through this sacrament to be able to love as he does. We need it to fight temptation and sin, to care for the needy, and to share the good news. We need his grace to survive and thrive in this world we live in.

But this Body and Bread we eat in the Eucharist is not only for today. It is for eternity. That's what Jesus promises: if we eat this bread, we will live forever. How could we not live forever, if Jesus' very own life is flowing through us? It is his life in us that will endure, and we will as well because we have become one with him.

That's the great gift of Jesus, the Bread of Life. The Eucharist is not something we can take for granted or think we can do without. Jesus asks us to believe that he is the One foreshadowed in the Old Testament, the One who rescues us from the slavery of sin, just as the Israelites were rescued from slavery in Egypt. He is the One who sustains us on our journey to the Promised Land, just as the Israelites were sustained by the manna in the wilderness. He is the One who will embrace us on that day when we reach the heavenly Promised Land, and we will know him because we have his life within us. That's the future he has promised to us who believe!

Questions for Reflection and Discussion

1. Have you ever experienced a time in which something from your past helped you to understand an experience of your present? How does widening your eyes to look to the past help you to appreciate the present?

2. Do you believe that God wants the best for you? Just as he provided manna for the Israelites in the desert, how has he demonstrated his faithfulness in your life so far?

3. What are your hopes and dreams for the future? How does your past affect your vision of the future? Are you looking forward to eternal life with God in heaven?

4. How often do you envision God's life flowing through you when you receive Communion? How does the grace you receive in the Eucharist affect your day-to-day life?

5. How would a greater awareness of God's desire to give you his life change how often you receive the Lord in Eucharist?

Before the Next Session

This week, take some time to write out the story of your relationship with God. It doesn't have to be extravagant (you could write it out "shorthand" or in bulleted points), but do strive to answer the following questions:

- **How has your relationship with God grown so far?** How has he provided for you, and how have you loved and served him in response?

- **How is your relationship with God currently?** How would you still like it to grow? Where in your life do you need his grace?

This Sunday, carry these answers to Christ as you approach him in the Eucharist. As you recount your relationship with him, thank him for all that he has done in your life so far, and ask him for whatever you need for the future. As you do so, keep in mind that this is the moment you will be the most intimately united with him this side of eternity.

SESSION THREE

God's Faithful, Covenant Love

Luke 22:14-20

When the hour came, he took his place at table with the apostles. He said to them, "I have eagerly desired to eat this Passover with you before I suffer, for, I tell you, I shall not eat it [again] until there is fulfillment in the kingdom of God." Then he took a cup, gave thanks, and said, "Take this and share it among yourselves; for I tell you [that] from this time on I shall not drink of the fruit of the vine until the kingdom of God comes." Then he took the bread, said the blessing, broke it, and gave it to them, saying, "This is my body, which will be given for you; do this in memory of me." And likewise the cup after they had eaten, saying, "This cup is the new covenant in my blood, which will be shed for you."

Matthew 26:26-28

While they were eating, Jesus took bread, said the blessing, broke it, and giving it to his disciples said, "Take and eat; this is my body." Then he took a cup, gave thanks, and gave it to them, saying, "Drink from it, all of you, for this is my blood of the covenant, which will be shed on behalf of many for the forgiveness of sins."

"Embrace the insanity," my wife often reminds me. Her sage wisdom comes to mind at each family meal. It's amazing how, as a parent, you spend the first couple of years begging your kids to walk and talk and the next sixteen pleading with them to sit down and be quiet.

But although our family meals can be crazy, loud, and stressful, they are a true gift. When we sit down together and give thanks and break bread, we also break open the joys and struggles of our lives. This is a treasure worth protecting and a moment worth cherishing.

It is precisely through such an interaction—a family meal—that God foreshadows, and then reveals, his great gift of the Eucharist to us. The Last Supper is the most famous meal in human history, but its roots are found well over a thousand years earlier, in the time of Moses.

Passover was (and is) the most important feast of the Jewish calendar. Celebrated annually, Passover commemorates the Israelites' escape from slavery in Egypt. During the tenth plague in Exodus, God prescribed a way for his people to be protected from death. He ordered every household to select a lamb, slaughter it, eat its flesh, and cover the wooden doorpost of their home with the lamb's blood. (You can read about this in detail in Exodus 12.) That night the angel of death came and *passed over* any home with the blood of the lamb on its door. Without that blood, the firstborn male child of that household died (12:29).

The New Covenant

With this background in place, we can now turn to the Gospel account of the Last Supper. Jesus and the twelve disciples have gathered in the upper room to celebrate the Passover. The Exodus story will be retold. They will sing psalms, eat the lamb along with unleavened bread and bitter herbs, and remember God's faithfulness to their ancestors.

Then Jesus announces that there will be a "new covenant" (Luke 22:20). After the Israelites had crossed the Red Sea and traveled into the desert, God made a covenant with the people through Moses. He promised to protect the Israelites and nurture them, and they promised to abide by his commandments and be his special people.

But now God will make a new covenant with his people—a covenant of mercy lived under the law of love and in the joy of the Holy Spirit. It will be sealed not with the blood of an animal but with the blood of his beloved son. *Jesus* will be the lamb that will be sacrificed. The Passover celebration that began in the upper room with the Last Supper will end on the cross of Calvary—our doorway to heaven in the next life, and to hope and freedom in this life.

> God is so filled with love for us that he offers us this gift not once but weekly—even daily!

We participate in this very same meal at every single Mass. The upper room of Holy Thursday is as close as the sanctuary of our local parish where we take part in the Eucharistic sacrifice. God is so filled with love for us that he offers us this gift not once but weekly—even daily! It is so fundamental to our happiness that Pope Benedict XVI could say, "Where is the source of Christian joy to be found if not in the Eucharist?" (Angelus, March 18, 2007).

So when you enter into the Father's house this Sunday, take the time to recall how faithful God is. He will never reject or abandon you. He went to unimaginable lengths—sacrificing his beloved Son—to show you how much he loves you. And he did it for you, personally.

Our only response can be to give him thanks and praise. Perhaps that's why the Greek word for "thanksgiving" is *eucharistia,* because the family has come together to give thanks. This family meal is literally a gift from heaven.

Questions for Reflection and Discussion

1. What do you think of when you hear the word "covenant"? What other words convey the same meaning? What does this show you about who God is, that he would make a covenant with his people?

2. What difference does receiving the Eucharist make for you during the rest of the week? If you've ever missed Sunday Mass, for whatever reason, did you find yourself lacking in some way? Why or why not?

3. How have you seen God's faithfulness play out in your life? How does this help you trust in his faithful, covenant love in whatever challenges you are facing right now?

4. How often are you able to attend daily Mass? In what ways does it enrich your relationship with God?

5. Why do you think it was necessary for God to sacrifice his Son? How does that knowledge change the way you view the sacrifices you make in your own life for others?

Before the Next Session

1. Read the accounts of the Last Supper in Luke 22 and Matthew 26. Imagine being with Jesus and the disciples at table with them. What would the mood be? How would the disciples react to Jesus' words about his body and blood?

2. At Mass, we give thanks to God for his faithful, covenant love. Spend some time in prayer giving thanks to God for all the ways he has shown his love to you. Perhaps you could make a list. Include not only the big things you are grateful for but also all the little ways in which he shows that he loves you. Then bring your list to Mass on Sunday, and read it over after you've received Jesus in the Eucharist. Allow your own heart to swell in gratitude and love for all that he has done for you. Ask him to give you the grace to remember his constant, unending love for you as you "Go in peace, glorifying the Lord by your life."

SESSION FOUR

Jesus Is Walking with You

Luke 24:28-31

As they approached the village to which they were going, he gave the impression that he was going on farther. But they urged him, "Stay with us, for it is nearly evening and the day is almost over." So he went in to stay with them. And it happened that, while he was with them at table, he took bread, said the blessing, broke it, and gave it to them. With that their eyes were opened and they recognized him, but he vanished from their sight.

When I was sixteen years old, I went on a month-long wilderness trip through Montana, Wyoming, and Oregon. For a kid raised in the Sonora Desert of Arizona, it was life changing. I had never seen such open spaces filled with so much life. The landscape was breathtaking and the air, pristine. We fell asleep each night under a sky blanketed with stars—more stars than I had ever seen before.

One night our adult guides sat with us and began to point out specific constellations. I was fascinated. It was as though I had looked at these shiny starry "dots" in the sky night after night but couldn't truly appreciate them until someone "connected the dots" for me.

I recall that scene often when I read or hear Luke's story about the two disciples on the road to Emmaus. The two disciples are walking from Jerusalem to a village called Emmaus, about seven miles away. They are downtrodden. They had hoped that Jesus "would be the one to redeem Israel" (Luke 24:21). They were not the only ones. Following Jesus' crucifixion, those who had closely followed him were distraught, believing that his death meant that he was not the Messiah who was promised by God and foretold in prophecy. They did not expect Jesus to be powerless and to submit to a humiliating death on the cross.

Jesus himself draws near and asks the travelers about their "story." Prevented from recognizing him, the disciples do not know who is actually joining them on their journey. Jesus asks what they are discussing. They begin to recount all that has happened. In doing so, they reveal not only their broken hearts but also their broken hopes and dreams, now dead and buried with their beloved rabbi from Nazareth. (Notice how Jesus takes an interest in them *and* in their suffering.)

After listening to them, Jesus then weaves together story after story from the Scriptures, offering context and perspective on who he is and why he had to die. In effect, he was "connecting the dots" for them. But the final connection comes when they sit down to have dinner. In the breaking of the bread, he reveals his true presence as the risen Christ. This is far beyond anything the two disciples could have ever hoped for or imagined possible.

This story shows us two important truths. First, Christ is present to us even when we don't "recognize" that he is there. He is the One who comes to us, especially in moments of sorrow and suffering. Jesus does not abandon us in our moments of trial—he draws near; he walks alongside us. He constantly meets us where we are and guides us to where he desires us to be. He will travel to the ends of the earth to be with us. He is constantly reaching out to us, if we only have the eyes of faith to see it.

> He constantly meets us where we are and guides us to where he desires us to be.

Second, Jesus is most present to us in the Eucharist. He has stopped at nothing to be close to us, even coming in the flesh under the simplest "disguises" of bread and wine. So even when we don't sense God's presence, we know without a doubt that he is truly with us, body, blood, soul, and divinity, in the Eucharist.

Like the two disciples on the road to Emmaus, we can encounter the risen Christ in the breaking of the bread. This too is a gift beyond our wildest hopes and dreams. The God of the universe, who has forgiven all our sins, has not just made himself present on the altar for us to adore at a distance. When we consume him, we take him into our body, heart, and mind. He comes as close to us as possible this side of heaven.

Questions for Reflection and Discussion

1. How can a practice of "connecting the dots" benefit you and your faith life? What is one example of a time when the dots were connected for you and you gained a more holistic perspective of your situation?

2. Do you invite Christ into your journey by talking to him about your pain, sorrow, and joys? Why or why not? What happens when you do?

3. Have you ever struggled with believing that Jesus is really present in the Eucharist? If so, what has helped you believe? If not, how would you share your belief in the Real Presence with someone who has doubts?

4. Share about a time when you may have felt as if God was absent in your life, perhaps as you were going through a difficult trial. How did you get through it? How did Mass and Holy Communion help you?

5. Take some time to read the Emmaus story right now, found in Luke 24:13-35. Contemplate or discuss what struck you. Does anything in this story directly relate to your life right now? Explain.

Before the Next Session

In the time of Moses, the presence and glory of God dwelt within a sacred meeting tent called the Tabernacle (from the Latin word *tabernaculum,* meaning "tent"). The tent sat in the middle of the camp during the Israelites' wanderings in the desert as a reminder that they were to keep the Lord at the center of their lives.

God told Moses how he wanted the tent and its contents designed. Our churches and sanctuaries are still patterned after the original tabernacle/tent, and the tabernacles of our parishes today still contain the presence and glory of God in the Holy Eucharist as Jesus continues to dwell among us (John 1:14).

This week, use the flickering red sanctuary candle to remind yourself that Christ is indeed fully present in that place. Specifically, you can acknowledge his presence with great regard and care by striving to do these few things:

1. Arrive early to pray quietly.
2. Genuflect as you reverence the presence of Christ in the tabernacle.
3. Fully participate in listening to the word of God with more than just your ears—with your head and your heart.
4. Pay attention to the meaning of each prayer that is prayed, and respond with sincerity.

SESSION FIVE

A Eucharistic Encounter

Mark 9:23-24

Jesus said to him, "'If you can!' Everything is possible to one who has faith." Then the boy's father cried out, "I do believe, help my unbelief!"

Ephesians 2:10

For we are his handiwork, created in Christ Jesus for the good works that God has prepared in advance, that we should live in them.

Galatians 2:20

Yet I live, no longer I, but Christ lives in me; insofar as I now live in the flesh, I live by faith in the Son of God who has loved me and given himself up for me.

The year was 1244, and Emperor Frederick II of Rome was at war with the pope. The emperor sent his armies throughout Italy and planned to attack several Catholic communities, including the small town of Assisi. St. Clare was quite ill and confined to a bed in her convent. But when news of the invading army reached her cell, she asked the priest to bring the Eucharist to her in a monstrance—the vessel used to hold the Eucharist during Adoration.

Clare prayed fervently before the Lord. Then, with newfound strength, she rose from her bed "armed" only with the Lord. As hundreds of trained soldiers began to surround the convent and approach its towering walls, St. Clare stood on the roof and elevated the monstrance containing the Blessed Sacrament. "I beseech thee, Good Lord," she prayed, "protect these whom now I am not able to protect!"

At that moment, the invaders stopped dead in their tracks, and their faces became almost ghostly white. As if they had been struck by lightning, the soldiers fell back from the walls.

This story illustrates several profound truths about the Eucharist. First, Jesus in the Eucharist gives us strength—maybe even strength we didn't know we had. St. Clare was very ill, and yet she was able to get up from her bed and face the challenge in front of her. With God's life flowing through us, we can find the strength to do what God is calling us to do, whether that's being a good parent, caring for a loved one, or fighting temptation and sin.

And that leads us to a second truth. Through the grace we receive, the Eucharist offers us protection—protection from the "wickedness and snares of the devil," as we say in the prayer to St. Michael the Archangel, as well as protection from the temptations we battle each day—temptations from the world and our own flesh.

Just as the Eucharist had the power to save Assisi from the invading forces, it has the power to save and protect us from our own weaknesses and sins. We just have to believe. If we struggle with believing that the Eucharist can really do that for us, then we can cry out with the father whose child needed the Lord's healing power: "I do believe, help my unbelief!" (Mark 9:24).

Eucharistic Encounters

In these last four sessions, we have talked about the ways in which Jesus blesses us in the Eucharist. He pours his life into us. He showers us with his faithful, covenant love. He desires to have an intimate relationship with us. He walks beside us. He gives us strength and protects us from evil. All these blessings are available to us as we draw closer to Jesus in the Blessed Sacrament.

> With God's life flowing through us, we can find the strength to do what God is calling us to do.

So what are some ways you could spend time with Jesus outside of Sunday Mass? Perhaps you can rearrange your schedule to make it to a daily Mass one day. Or maybe you could stop by your parish chapel for Adoration and spend time in the presence of the Lord. God uses these encounters to pour more of his life, his love, and his strength into us, readying us to go back into the world "armed" with all we need, to do whatever he is calling us to do.

A Living Monstrance

If you've been to Adoration or a Eucharistic procession, you know what a monstrance looks like. The word comes from the Latin expression *monstrare*, meaning "to show." The next time you see it, notice that it's designed to display God's presence to the world. Often it's designed so that it appears as if rays of light are coming forth from the

Eucharistic center. This is intentional, meant to demonstrate the fact that Christ's glory is shining forth to the world.

Now consider this: you are like that monstrance. You are "wonderfully made" by God (Psalm 139:14). You are "his handiwork" (Ephesians 2:10). You have the presence of God within you (Galatians 2:20). When you are filled with the Eucharist, you, like the monstrance, can most perfectly fulfill the purpose for which you were designed (Jeremiah 1:4-8).

The *Catechism* says the Eucharist is "the source and summit of the Christian life" (1324). So make Jesus the center of your life. It is only then that life makes sense. It is only then that you can allow Christ's light to shine forth from you to everyone you encounter each day.

Questions for Reflection and Discussion

1. Do you ever struggle to believe that the Eucharist has the power to transform and save you? Why or why not? Have you seen any changes in yourself since beginning this study?

2. What areas of your life do you feel you don't have the energy or strength to change or carry out? How could the Eucharist strengthen you to do whatever God is calling you to do?

3. Would you say that Jesus is at the center of your life? In what ways? How could you make your relationship with him even more of a priority?

4. How might you already be a "living monstrance" to others? How would you like to shine with Christ's light even more?

5. How can you reorder your life to make it to daily Mass or to Adoration of the Blessed Sacrament during the course of the week?

For Your Life . . .

Regular time spent with the Lord in the Eucharist can be life changing. In the silence of a quiet church, you can talk to him about what's on your mind—and he can tell you what's on his. He can pour out his love on you and help you to see where you need to change. Here are some ways to make this form of prayer a regular part of your life:

- **Be real with yourself.** If you're not used to working out every day, you probably won't go to the gym and expect to exercise for an hour. Holy hours are great, but you might need to build up to it. Start with going to the chapel for fifteen minutes at a time. The quality of time you spend with our Lord and the frequency of times are often more meaningful than the length.

- **Stay practical.** It might not be realistic for you to get over to your church whenever you feel like it. Perhaps you live some distance from your parish, or your schedule just doesn't allow for it. Maybe you can arrive early to Mass and spend some time with Jesus. Or maybe you could arrange your schedule so that you (and even a spouse, child, or friend with you) can stop in as you're driving past the church on your way to school or to the grocery store. Even a few minutes can drastically change your week for the better.

- **Go out of your way.** Once you get into the habit of spending time with the Lord in the Eucharist, look at your calendar and think bigger. When can you get there that might not be as convenient? How can you make your Adoration time such a regular part of your weekly rhythm of prayer that other things, such as time online or watching TV, are sacrificed to ensure you have more time with the Lord? Start searching for more opportunities to sacrifice other things for that prayer time with Jesus—and watch how he blesses you.

Like anything else that is worthwhile in life, it takes a certain degree of discipline to become more Eucharistic in your prayer life. Remember, however, that God is never outdone in generosity.

✝ More in This Series

Getting More Out of Prayer
by Patricia Mitchell
Prayer is where we meet with God and grow in a relationship with him. Deepen your connection with the Lord through weekly reflections and prayer exercises.

Getting More Out of Mass
by Fr. John Muir
Sometimes life's cares, hard-to-understand readings, and even not-so-great music can distract us from what Jesus wants to give us in the Mass. Fr. John Muir provides reflections to help you get the most out of Mass.

Getting More Out of Confession
by Joel Stepanek
Experience the Sacrament of Reconciliation as an encounter with love and mercy itself. In this booklet, Joel Stepanek invites you to welcome Jesus, the Divine Physician, to heal your heart.

Getting More Out of Lent
by Deacon Keith Strohm
Do you dread the season of Lent? It doesn't have to be that way. Come to know God in a deeper and more personal way this Lent.

GET THE MOST OUT OF YOUR BOOKLET

Before each session, visit **wau.org/faithseries** for a short video from the author.

the WORD
among us®
The *Spirit* of Catholic Living

This book was published by The Word Among Us. Since 1981, The Word Among Us has been answering the call of the Second Vatican Council to help Catholic laypeople encounter Christ in the Scriptures.

The name of our company comes from the prologue to the Gospel of John and reflects the vision and purpose of all of our publications: to be an instrument of the Spirit, whose desire is to manifest Jesus' presence in and to the children of God. In this way, we hope to contribute to the Church's ongoing mission of proclaiming the gospel to the world so that all people would know the love and mercy of our Lord and grow more deeply in their faith as missionary disciples.

Our monthly devotional magazine, *The Word Among Us*, features meditations on the daily and Sunday Mass readings and currently reaches more than one million Catholics in North America and another half million Catholics in one hundred countries around the world. Our book division, The Word Among Us Press, publishes numerous books, Bible studies, and pamphlets that help Catholics grow in their faith.

To learn more about who we are and what we publish, visit us at www.wau.org. There you will find a variety of Catholic resources that will help you grow in your faith.

Embrace His Word, Listen to God . . .

www.wau.org